mid-life

poems by

Ana Maria Caballero

Finishing Line Press
Georgetown, Kentucky

mid-life

ACKNOWLEDGMENTS

The following poems have been previously published:

Alliteration Magazine, "How Others Do It"
Aviary Review, "A Notion of Marriage"
Big River Poetry Review, "The Public"
Boston Poetry Review, "The Clothes Maker"
Clamor, "Mercury, Retrograde" and "The Hour of the Star is Here"
The East Bay Review, "Revel"
Empty Mirror Books, "The Stories of Bedtime"
Ghost House Review, "Morning Feed"
Pea River Review, "Differences" and "Yellow Tomatoes"
The Potomac, "The Open Dishwasher" and "Sick Talk"
Really Systems, "Another Airport Poem"
Red Savina Review, "The Suffering Game"
Smoking Glue Gun Magazine, "Paco"

Publisher: Leah Maines

Editor: Christen Kincaid

Cover Art: Rolando Adrian Avila

Author Photo: Juan Rivas

Cover Design: Elizabeth Maines

Printed in the USA on acid-free paper.
Order online: www.finishinglinepress.com
also available on amazon.com

Author inquiries and mail orders:
Finishing Line Press
P. O. Box 1626
Georgetown, Kentucky 40324

Table of Contents

*To Nelson David, my partner in
mid-life*

THE OPEN DISHWASHER

Today, you fell face first into the open dishwasher

One plastic prong bruised your nose
Another gave you your first black eye

I rushed to cradle you
And sing your falling down song

Then I took you outside to show you
The birds, the lizards
The cloudless blue sky
And the moon, your moon, visible today at noon

The moon made you calm
Luna, luna you said
And pointed up
At the cloudless blue sky

I sat you down close to me
Ready to hold you
If you still needed my arms

But you looked at the white powder moon
At a lizard that dashed from the bush
And at crests of neat waves rise from the pool

After a moment, you sighed
Your first veteran sigh

Just yesterday
I checked the classifieds
For work I might be paid to complete

I do this sometimes
To confirm I remain hireable
And am more than some lullaby mother

Who sits with her child
To be soothed by the moon

REVEL
For Dr. S. Rueda

On the night Chavez died
I needed to feel drunk
So I called my son's pediatrician
Told him I wanted to be happy
He said I should be happy
I didn't mention the wine
Maybe he figured and it wasn't the first time
First I mixed white formula with water
Then drank enough to sway
With the people on TV
Even a teat gets tired
Of being just a teat

MORNING FEED

You are a great round thing in my arms
Each morning

I unwrap you to make you cold
And warm you myself

Eat child drink only the good
While you still can

Unknowing small pale and perfect
We become

As you take from me the only self
I have to give

ISADORA

Isadora Duncan was certainly raped
I still want my daughter to shelter her name
Isadora Duncan's kids drowned in the Seine
I still want my daughter to salvage her name
Isadora Duncan lived on her toes and they bled
I still want my daughter to harbor her name
Isadora Duncan's bed was left unmade
I still want my daughter to inhabit her name
Isadora Duncan twirled a scarf into a neck
I will ask my daughter to relish her name

AND IF IT'S A GIRL

Must I teach her this   life
Of precision within
And democracy   throughout

Must I scrub her face with   the rules
Of biology and skin
Of ambition and   kid

Must she learn   the empty errand look
Reign in a fucking passion for shoes
Gorge air   digest age

Must she commit to   perfume
Paint her mouth into a button
Wield a plot to dress a   room

And once the future is   her womb
Will she, too, hope to beget
Another belly boy   balloon

THE STORIES OF BEDTIME

I am the only mother
And you are the only son

Your father
He, too, is the only father
       The only man

His father and my father
Are past fathers
       Stories to tell you
Of men
Who once walked

My mother and his mother
A photograph and a portrait
We point to
Upon the wall

You will have a sister
And she will be the only daughter

I a daughter of the painted tales
Father will read you
To remember when it was
       Our time

SUNBLOCK

If I ever were to bake a cake
it would be for you,
and I'd color in the icing
like spreading sunblock on your face.

I like to get you while you sleep—
the best is in a car—
so I can butter every toe
and beneath your pillow feet.

Underneath your feet because
at the beach you will crawl
then turn back up and hook a foot
in the elbow of your jaw.

Sometimes you fart, snore or sigh—
show me you approve
of the cold sunscreen I rub
onto your miniature thigh.

I get there's grace to growing old
each time a rim of white
forms a stencil from your ear
and records your neck's fat rolls.

Daddy speaks from the front seat,
bids to leave you still.
Oh, but your fresh bread hands,
and you sleep, and I don't hear.

THE GOOD LIFE

We get off the plane—

I browse online
Find the shirt he wants to buy

We go to dinner
Consider the baby girl we hope to have

Once we are full, he helps me rise
In this life, I may never write—

MEANTIME

In the morning, I adjust my goals.

Some are satisfied, others
Unmet. We stare.

Meditate every day.
A happy hour with the team.
Find a publisher.

I touch upon each line like I first
Touched the eyes of cold dead fish,
Mother in front, selecting
The fish her family would soon eat.

It is late August. Another year gone by.
Dead fish eyes jellify beneath each unmet line.

Yet, the choices remain mine—

To write from countries larger than home
And soak in the tub
With my husband and son.

I will not speak of twenty years tendered
To one thing. Devotion ends
With a hop atop the airport train.

In the life I choose,
          I travel this   far.

BATHROOM TALK

Watching you pee in front of me while we talk about not being late
It's true we shouldn't be late to things
I try to remember when we began peeing and talking
In front of each other
I wish I could remember
I would tell you
I wish I had to pee
So that I could test you and see if you look
See if you question
Any less
What I am about to say
Which is basically
Everyone already expects us to be late
So maybe we altogether just stopped being late

A NOTION OF MARRIAGE

Because I am a poet,
I read about things like the center of skin.
About warm bodies coming together in the dark,
and how it can be the meaning of life
when someone gets it right.

And I know I should write about things
like a moving chest and a naked back.
About the coming together of life in the dark,
about our common desire
and the verbs that it took.

And it should be universal,
but personal.
My moving chest, your naked back.
The notion of marriage,
of children, of daily love.
Shrinking rooms
beneath the surface
of different meaning words.

But I don't see the dark jaw
in the night,
or the soft center of touch spring alive.
There is effort and a plan.
There is marriage,
a shrinking room,
daily love,
and a baby that eats time.

We do not say flesh when we mean sex.
We say, "It's about right."
And, "It would be nice."
We confirm how long it's been
before we ask the other to get up
and make the bedroom
dark

ANOTHER AIRPORT POEM

No,
this is not about the sharing of caution.

This is merely about distance
and its reverse magnetism.
About the slow winding of a week's time
into the delicate tautness of a telephone line.
About the opposite windmilling of willing hands
powered by the windward breeze
that blows,
however softly,
on separate lands.

HOW OTHERS DO IT

Two idiots like us—
Who planned love like a new car

Who bought the floorboards old—
So with each step our new home moaned

Who mapped the lock—
And learned to speak fraternal talk

Who toiled to resist slog—
A balloon on our wrist in permanent bob

Who got drunk with the guests—
Painted like rage the right walls red

Who saw the new oven installed—
Where designer heat is focused and trapped

To roast the meat for today's avid son

GRADUAL ROT

Rot is a gradual process. It begins while the fruit is ripe and dangling from the tree. Once it falls, the process is in full, and the fruit must be thrown away or eaten quickly.

I have picked mangoes off the ground of warm places because they taste good when they are just about to turn bad. They are also delicious before they become ripe. Mangoes are an exception.

But, this is not about exceptions. This is about the gradual process of rot, even while clinging to a tree. Even while young and pleasant, with clean clothes and comfortable heels. Being mindful of the ground does not mean being ready for the fall.

T.S. ELIOT OR BUST

It was then:

The gauntlet,
the hatchet,
the atomic hammer hit of delete,
delete,
delete.

But I've done the yoga,
talked to people who know,
tasted acceptance, aged,
had children, left
home.

Death is coming, coming
whether I write about it
or not—
licking my dim heels
with its split, pink
tongue.

Here, there is no Pound
collecting cash for my free time.
No great sin, no absent father,
no ancient crime.
Mental illness lies near,
but it is not mine.

No politics. No poster,
no red siren call. I am shiftless,
ill at ease,
my voice climbs flat as a wall.
Woe is me

For I am the child who hits the pool,
grabs the side, finds the mother
and yells for help to do it again.
I am that mother who tells the father:
You, jump in the water.

Death is coming, coming
whether I write about it
or not—
licking my dim heels
with its split, pink
tongue.

It is now:

I am no Eliot
and this
this is no song.

These will never be pearls
that are my eyes.

So,
let us go
then
          (you and/or I)
to a fully loaded street
where our dim heels can rest
or have some fun.

PELICAN

On the third dive, I look.

A pelican's beak cracks the gray October sea.
The swish of water upon its body is the only sound,

save for a small fishing boat battling to start.

I drop what I am doing
and watch.

The bird extends a faucet neck,
slips a fish down its throat.
Its wings slide back in reverence,
          or hunger,
before flying off.

I notice, now, ripples in the water,
unrelated to the pelican-pierced bay.

Small fish defy big fish in an easy slosh
of broken waves.

Suddenly, the fishing boat darts.

I quit wondering if subaquatic death
takes a silent form for I, too,
          must work
to survive.

MASTER

All of a sudden, I have a new prayer.
Send me a master, please.
The baby you sent is everything.
Is teaching, yes.
But I can grow more, harder.
Give, so as to become.
Be humble, like you said.
Write it all down, for someone else.
Feel smaller, talk smaller.
Life is the speech inside my head, static.
I seek a changed phrase, a living word.
Unjudging and massive, gentle at night.
An open face to greet those you send, hi.
Hi, I pray.
Send me a master, amen.

FLIGHT PLAN

If the death of each person implies
A lesson claimed
A mission fulfilled

And a message conveyed
To the subsisting family

I must marvel at God's
Logistical planning
And baggage handling

Pilots and stewards
Coach and Economy Plus

In one swift transaction
All aboard the ocean floor
Frequent flyer club

THE PUBLIC

Born of the first stone, I am witch:
spellbound by small elements,
snails in the throat, birds on the lip.

There is a hiding behind the trunk
of a dead tree, a memory
of morning, a reckoning.

There are no men, no children.
No women with soft worries.
No confidences or shared will.

But when I blow the lonesome wind,
the wooded land breathes in.
Together we become the ancient word,

a god released.

THE CLOTHES MAKER

My clothes come from places that are not immediately obvious—

A forty-day South American Christmas, an attempt at youth in college, a place of blessing turned hard.

Embroidering is slow, so I mix patience with excess and comfort. Embroidering can be silent or loud, and it is inside and out; but it remains the single piece of cloth I choose.

At unexpected sounds, my thread sheers a right breast pocket to gently cinch the waist. A set of green grapes spilled from the cup of an already full Caravaggio.

THE HOUR OF THE STAR IS HERE

To Clarice Lispector and her book "A hora da estrela" ("The Hour of the Star")

As the author, I alone love you.
If you don't get a call, it is because I have your phone.
The others are busy calling each other, being each other.
I made them that way, but it is you who wants revenge.
It is you, child, who has a gut.
Take that red lipstick, this sugared cup of coffee, as your own.
See my white hand draw them out for you, flat on your back.
There is no doctor who will work for free, no man.
There is me, love.
I am with you, here, where my lack of heart starts to hurt.

DIFFERENCES

The Modern Father insists upon grandmother's house. It is not his concern if we do not wish to be stilled by a room shelved with dust. The Postmodern Dad expects us to go because we enjoy shelved dust and finished lives hung round on picture frames.

I wanted to know this deliberately, like that, so I took the course. Did the reading I was raised to do. Drew her closer, the Woman who thinks of things like the Father through Time.

This is called having it all. All means the poem. The poem means emptied time. Emptied time means a father on the line asking if I've gone to tell his mother that he is getting better, almost doing fine.

THE SUN COAST

Father does not know he is in Cancelada.

Mother said dinner is fun and the boats are big in Puerto Banús.

We are taking Father to a hospital in Estepona.

Reservations for lunch await in a white restaurant in Mijas.

He fell last night in Ronda.

We must be patient; the doctor lives in Málaga.

A 24-hour pharmacy is open in San Pedro.

The greetings we'd send are ash in Marbella.

Gibraltar is closed anyway.

SICK TALK

My father's illness is so close I do not write about it. This is not writing about it. If I were writing about it, you would know. It would be about your father having a stroke and your mother closing her life. It would be about diapers and nurses and therapy. And about your mother opening her life to see if it is still closed.

More things must happen before I can make meaning out of the bad remembering. Right now, I remember it all, and I cannot write about it all. It would mean nothing to you, like my monologue for when people ask—

First, we talk about saying hello. Then we speak about my baby or their baby or yours. But, when street words run out, I am forced to summarize a sick father to shroud silence that never did anything wrong.

PACO

Last night, I heard Paco de Lucía play the guitar
in a theater cut out of a dry rock in the South of Spain.

My father could not go because he fell
and hit his head
and has been in bed for fifteen days
and it could be longer.

My brothers are not here and do not know.

So I went with my mother
to see men with faces that look like the first face,

the face of the Gypsy and the Jew,
the Arab sage and the hanging Christ.
Hair around the eyes,
a focusing view of enemy foot
through rising desert sand.

El Farru, the great flamenco dancer,
danced in the middle of the music men
and lost a dancing heel
in the middle of the song.

The dead heel lay dumb
like a bitten fig
while El Farru beat his sounding heel down.

Then he bowed
and held up his mute heel to make our hands applaud.

De Lucía. His nephew-apprentice to the left.
The singers with no voice, dry rock slicing their throats.
The bass that seized a place and played a role.
The flamenco hair whipping Farru's face
like a despot rider his despot horse.

I filmed it all to show my father.
But the clip will deepen
the slip of the heel and the dry rock
against the head.

So I keep it for my mother,
for when she'll need her music men.

THE ERRANDS OF DEATH

They are the errands of death that rout me—
the way the body will be removed from the house

The question of who will remain composed—
of how to summon the white contraption with wheels

In the elevator the body will not fit flat—
bound in a blanket, right side up

A brother to arrange the business of mass—
money exchanged so people can whimper in rows

Will he be cremated—
yes, of course

Then the ashes—
how to select which container to hold

MERCURY, RETROGRADE

Mother,
you've killed me with your emirate hand.
The flood you called momma love
soaked my art,
sent rapids through each tunnel dug.

Mother,
I fear the birth of a daughter.
Another to flood, to forge
with our white eel
discipline face.

It is so. It is all the same.
Momma's communist love,
Momma's tourniquet sway.

Mother,
thank you for the trip abroad.
There were mornings like pamphlets on joy,
but by noon
tongue-thrown flowers
doused the afternoon.

Mother,
your battle is agrarian.
Unfair my fertile lands.
Confused, I drew gift poorly,
your yoga left intact.

Momma, let's not abuse fault.

No word can exist
simply now—

Father just became

YELLOW TOMATOES

I once thought I could know anything

The death knowledge of the Buddha
The clarifying call of Gabriel
Former lives and abetting suns
That enthrall worlds more able than mine

I too never doubted my time supply
To be the daughter to the dying father
Who buries without the blow of love regret

But my father is dying an excessive death
With a wounded body
That aligns rare moments of life
To the faint efforts of his mind

And I do

I offer my happy baby's dance
Ask about our mayor and the bad president
So together
We can wave our related heads with a laugh

I bring home the foods he likes to eat
Chocolate sugar-free
A bag of sweet yellow tomatoes
That falls when his good hand forgets to grab

And when he insists on phoning my mother
Makes a promise that he won't speak drink
I dial

I do I dance

Far from the Buddha knowledge of the giving death
Deaf to the recurring chant of Gabriel
Books by my bed and worlds of grace
That I grasp
But lack the good hand with which to grab

THE SUFFERING GAME

Mother wins the suffering game
        She cares for the sick

Big Brother is the runner up
He pays for the sick and for Mother to live better than sick
Only his Mondays count

Little Brother plays a private suffering game
And is left alone to tend his odds

I lose the suffering game
My baby is a balloon smile and his father
Loves us every day with capable hands

As the loser of the game
I am given a brick to hang from my face

In this small way I help bring life
        Something closer to fair

Ana **Maria Caballero** is a Colombian writer living in Miami. In 2014, her book *Entre domingo y domingo* (*From Sunday to Sunday*) won Colombia's José Manuel Arango National Poetry Prize and received second prize in the *Ediciones Embalaje* nationwide contest. Her work has appeared in over twenty journals, including *Smoking Glue Gun Magazine*, *Red Savina Review*, *Jai-Alai Magazine*, *CutBank* and *The Potomac*. She often writes about poetry for *Zeteo Journal*. Harvard University awarded her a *magna cum laude* Bachelor's degree for spending four years reading the world's best French, Spanish and Italian literature. Madrid's Complutense University offered her a scholarship to research her honors thesis work on café life in *fin de siècle* Paris and Barcelona, which she did, *in situ*. Together with her husband, she is a grateful parent to Lorenzo and Nina Isadora. Ana's poems and book thoughts can be found at thedrugstorenotebook.co.